CARS

Written by Ian Graham
Illustrated by Mick Gillah

RSVP
RAINTREE
STECK-VAUGHN
PUBLISHERS
The Steck-Vaughn Company

Austin, Texas

© Copyright 1994, Steck-Vaughn Company

Editor: Frank Tarsitano
Project Manager: Julie Klaus

Library of Congress Cataloging-in-Publication Data
Graham, Ian 1953-.
      Cars / written by Ian Graham; illustrated by Mick Gillah.
         p.   cm. — (Pointers)
      Includes index.
      Summary: Brief text and labeled illustrations discuss the characteristics and uses of different types of automobiles, including sport cars, family sedans, racing cars, all-terrain vehicles, and vans.
      ISBN 0-8114-6162-9
      1. Automobiles — Juvenile literature.   [1. Automobiles.]
I. Gillah, Mick, Ill.   II. Title.   III. Series.
TL147.G66   1994
629.22—dc20   93-19707
                            CIP
                            AC

Printed and bound in the United States

1 2 3 4 5 6 7 8 9 0 VH 99 98 97 96 95 94 93

Foreword

This book is about the different types of cars that are driven on racetracks, rally courses, and public roads. They include sports cars, family sedans, racing cars, and multipurpose vehicles.

All cars have certain features in common. They all have four wheels, an engine, and a body. But different types of cars are designed to be used for different purposes. Formula One racing cars must be fast to win races. Rally cars have to be able to grip loose surfaces as they speed down country roads. Sports cars are sleek, fast, and fun to drive. All-terrain, or sports utility vehicles have to be able to drive over rough ground. Multipurpose cars and vans need lots of room inside for passengers and luggage. Family sedans need to be comfortable on long journeys. Some cars combine power and luxury. These cars are usually called super cars.

Cars have to be safe, too. Racing and rally cars have to be especially strong to protect their drivers from accidents at high speeds. More cars now have computers which help control the brakes. The computers help to stop cars from skidding out of control. This book looks inside all these types of cars.

Contents

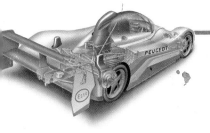

Small Hatchback

When the cost of gasoline rose steeply in the 1970s, carmakers began designing smaller cars with smaller engines that would use less gasoline. These smaller cars are popular because of their low running costs and because their small size also makes them easier to park, especially in busy towns. Many of these small cars are hatchbacks. Along with the usual doors on their sides, they also have a rear door, hinged at the top, that opens up a large loading area.

The Fiat Cinquecento 500 is a small three-door hatchback. It can carry up to five people and can drive for 500 miles (800 km) at a speed of 60 miles per hour (90 kph) on one tank of fuel.

4 A tenth of the car's weight is made from plastic materials that can be recycled (taken out of an old car and used to make parts for new cars).

Smooth body shape cuts air resistance

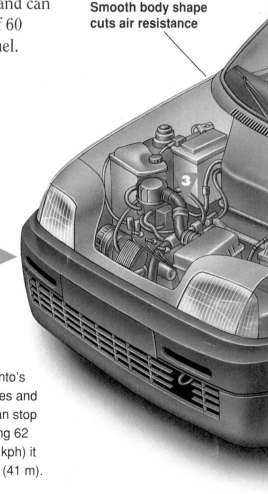

3 Most Cinquecentos have gas engines. One model comes with an electric motor instead of a gas engine. This electric car uses 12 batteries.

2 The deep front bumper with round edges is made from strong plastic. It is strong enough to withstand a small accident without breaking.

1 The Cinquecento's front disc brakes and rear drum brakes can stop the car quickly. Going 62 miles per hour (100 kph) it can stop in 135 feet (41 m).

5 The whole back of the car is a door that lifts upward and outward for easy loading. The rear seats fold down to fit in long loads.

6 The Cinquecento has one large door on each side that opens wide to make it easier for passengers to get in and out of the rear seats.

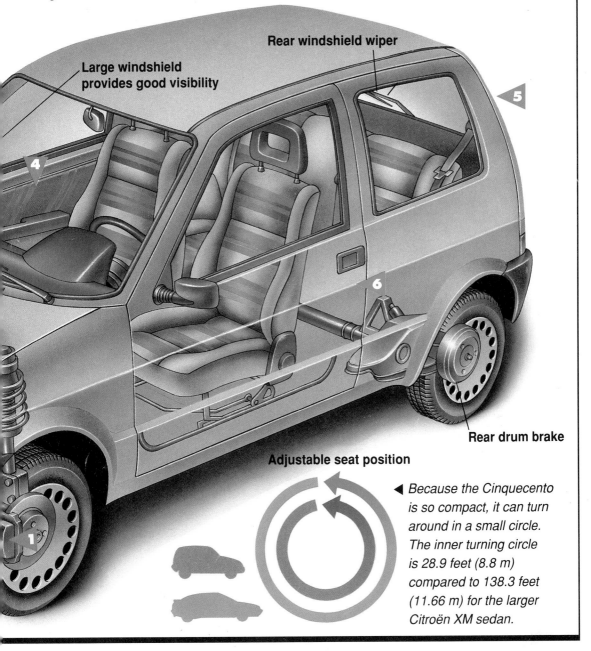

Rear windshield wiper

Large windshield provides good visibility

Rear drum brake

Adjustable seat position

◄ *Because the Cinquecento is so compact, it can turn around in a small circle. The inner turning circle is 28.9 feet (8.8 m) compared to 138.3 feet (11.66 m) for the larger Citroën XM sedan.*

Family Sedan

The modern family sedan is a comfortable, quiet car. It is big enough to carry a family and all its luggage. Different sizes and types of engines are often made for the same car. The number of doors also varies — there are usually two, three, four, or five doors.

The French Citroën XM is a large, five-door family sedan with enough space for five people. Its advanced suspension system helps give a comfortable ride so that the driver and passengers can relax on long journeys.

2 The XM is a very safe car. The car's reinforced body protects passengers from injury in case of an accident.

3 A computer controls the heating and cooling system. The car is comfortable inside even if the temperature is very cold or very hot outside.

1 The XM can have one of four different engines. One of the engines burns diesel oil instead of gasoline.

4 The aerodynamic shape of the XM cuts down air resistance to save fuel.

5 A screen behind the rear seats protects the passengers from drafts or engine fumes when the rear door is opened.

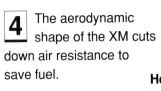

Heated rear window prevents fogging

Spoiler (wing) smooths airflow over rear

Childproof locks stop children from opening rear doors.

A computer checks the XM's suspension five times every second. As the car goes over bumps, the suspension is adjusted to give a smooth ride. Five sensors constantly monitor the car and how it is being driven.

Luxurious leather seats

6 The position of the front seats can be changed automatically in six different ways.

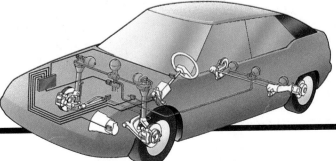

► Station Wagon

Some people need a car that provides more space than either a hatchback or a family sedan. For them, many cars are made in an extra-large version called a station wagon. These cars have much more space in the back for carrying cargo. There is a large door at the rear of the car (the tailgate) that lifts up so that cargo can be loaded and unloaded easily.

The Volvo 960 station wagon is a larger version of the Volvo 960 four-door sedan.

2 The driver's seat position can be changed by pressing a button. A computer memory stores three different positions.

Tailgate

Disc brake

VOLVO

1 An extra seat large enough for two people can be added to the storage area at the back of the car. The Volvo 960 holds seven people.

3 A strong body frame is designed to protect the passengers inside in case of an accident. If the car is hit from the side, the force of the crash is spread throughout the car.

4 Like all station wagons, the Volvo 960 is a big, heavy car. It has a powerful six-cylinder, 24-valve engine, capable of pulling heavy loads.

5 An anti-lock braking system (ABS) enables the car to brake without skidding by releasing and reapplying the brakes many times every second.

6 The steering column is made in sections that collapse in a crash. This stops the driver from being trapped in the car by the steering wheel.

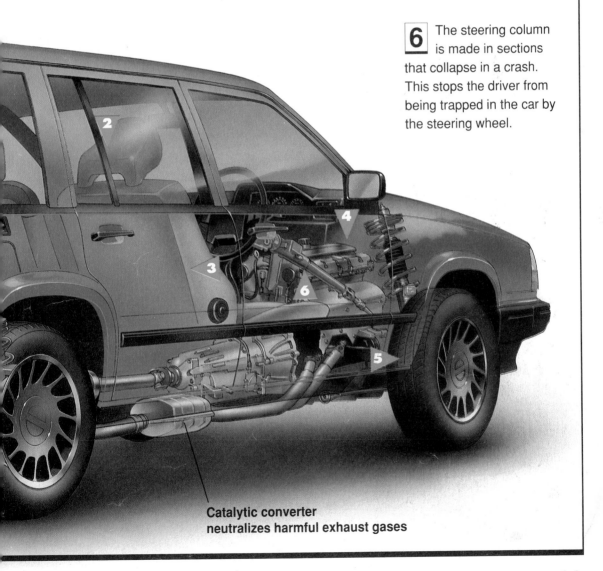

Catalytic converter neutralizes harmful exhaust gases

All-Terrain Vehicle

The Range Rover is a type of "all-terrain" vehicle. This means it can be driven on the road like other cars, but it is also designed to be driven over uneven, wet, or soft ground.

An ordinary car would soon become stuck in mud or damaged by rocks. The Range Rover is built with more space between its undercarriage and the ground than other cars have. This keeps the Range Rover clear of rough ground.

2 The Range Rover has a powerful engine. It can pull a trailer weighing up to 4 tons and can go at a speed of more than 100 miles per hour (170 kph).

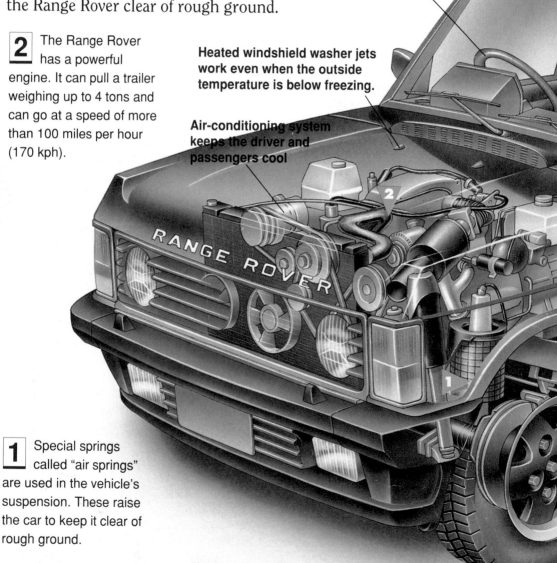

Power steering makes driving easier.

Heated windshield washer jets work even when the outside temperature is below freezing.

Air-conditioning system keeps the driver and passengers cool

1 Special springs called "air springs" are used in the vehicle's suspension. These raise the car to keep it clear of rough ground.

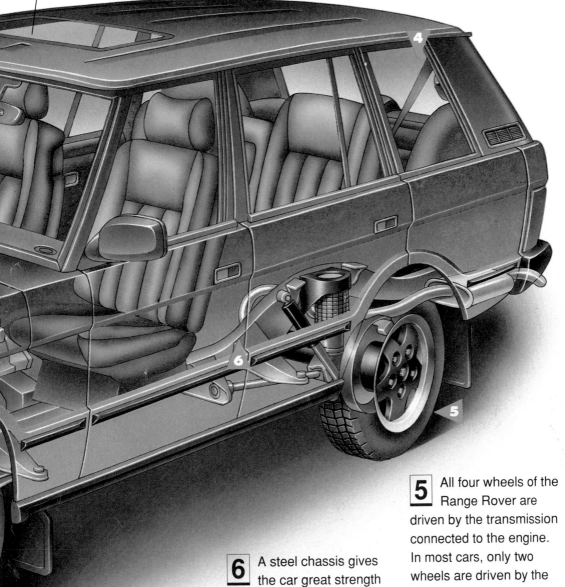

3 Most of the body panels are made from sheets of aluminum, a lightweight metal that does not rust.

4 A large tailgate (door) at the rear opens up to a storage area.

Electrically powered sunroof

5 All four wheels of the Range Rover are driven by the transmission connected to the engine. In most cars, only two wheels are driven by the transmission. All-wheel drive provides grip in dirt, mud, and snow.

6 A steel chassis gives the car great strength and stops it from bending when it is driven "off the road."

Multipurpose Van

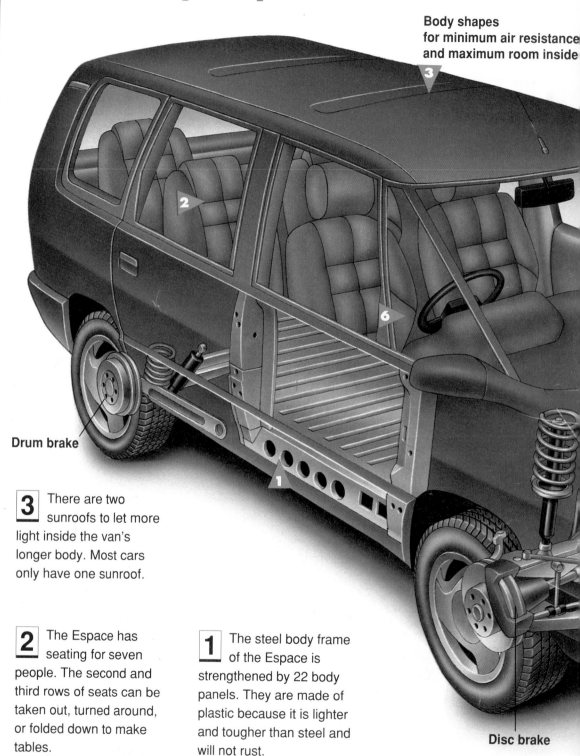

Body shapes
for minimum air resistance
and maximum room inside

Drum brake

Disc brake

3 There are two sunroofs to let more light inside the van's longer body. Most cars only have one sunroof.

2 The Espace has seating for seven people. The second and third rows of seats can be taken out, turned around, or folded down to make tables.

1 The steel body frame of the Espace is strengthened by 22 body panels. They are made of plastic because it is lighter and tougher than steel and will not rust.

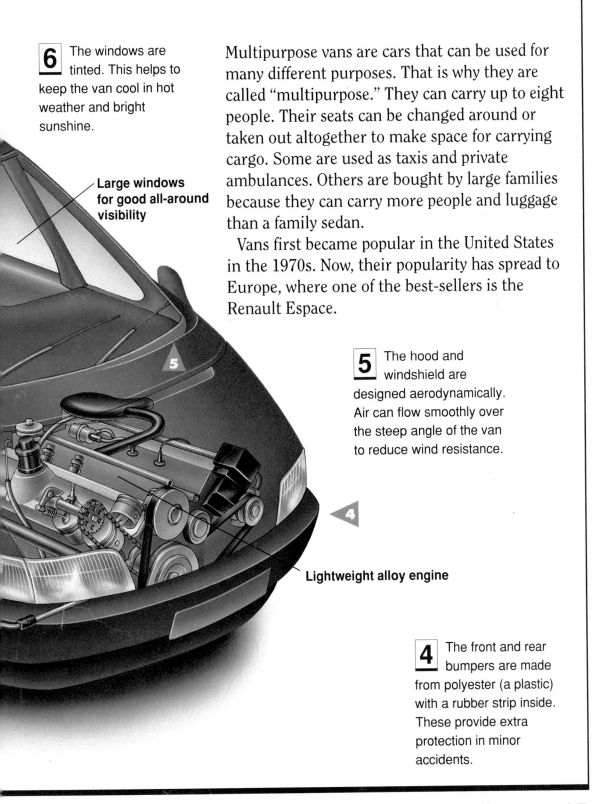

6 The windows are tinted. This helps to keep the van cool in hot weather and bright sunshine.

Large windows
for good all-around
visibility

Multipurpose vans are cars that can be used for many different purposes. That is why they are called "multipurpose." They can carry up to eight people. Their seats can be changed around or taken out altogether to make space for carrying cargo. Some are used as taxis and private ambulances. Others are bought by large families because they can carry more people and luggage than a family sedan.

Vans first became popular in the United States in the 1970s. Now, their popularity has spread to Europe, where one of the best-sellers is the Renault Espace.

5 The hood and windshield are designed aerodynamically. Air can flow smoothly over the steep angle of the van to reduce wind resistance.

Lightweight alloy engine

4 The front and rear bumpers are made from polyester (a plastic) with a rubber strip inside. These provide extra protection in minor accidents.

Luxury Sports Car

Some drivers want both the high speed and lively performance of a sports car and the comfortable and roomy surroundings of a sedan. For them, the luxury sports car gives the best of both worlds. It has the comfort of a sedan and the performance of a sports car. Luxury sports cars are very expensive, however.

The Mercedes 500SL is one of these luxury sports cars. It took 10 years to design. It can reach speeds of over 155 miles per hour (250 kph) while at the same time giving the driver and passengers a comfortable ride.

2 The side windows have double glazing for passenger comfort. Double glazing protects the compartment from outside noise and temperature.

Many of the plastic parts are designed to be recycled.

5-liter, 4-valves-per-cylinder engine

Broad air-intake grill helps to cool the engine

1 Both headlights have a mini-wiper to keep them clean and shining brightly. There are two extra lights built into the spoiler underneath the front bumper.

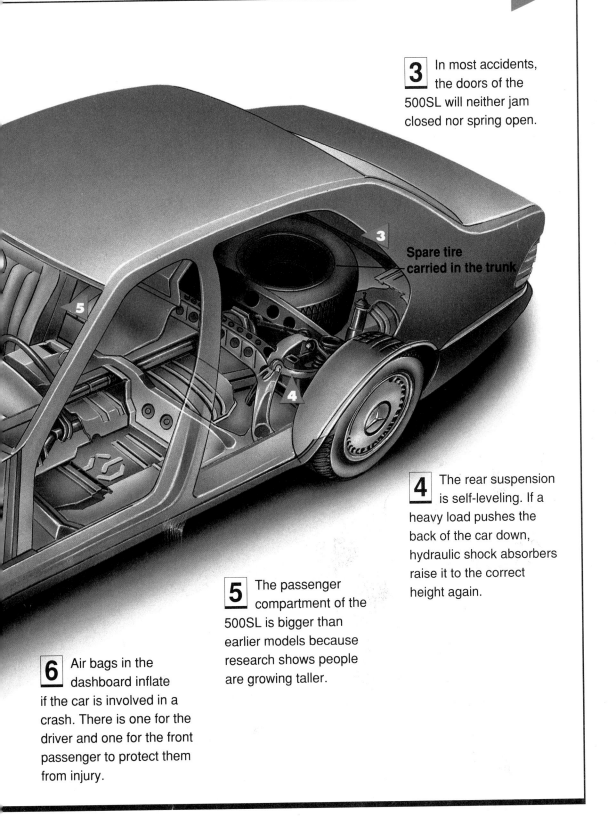

3 In most accidents, the doors of the 500SL will neither jam closed nor spring open.

3

Spare tire carried in the trunk

5

4

4 The rear suspension is self-leveling. If a heavy load pushes the back of the car down, hydraulic shock absorbers raise it to the correct height again.

5 The passenger compartment of the 500SL is bigger than earlier models because research shows people are growing taller.

6 Air bags in the dashboard inflate if the car is involved in a crash. There is one for the driver and one for the front passenger to protect them from injury.

Euro Sports Car

The Lotus Elan SE is a sports car with a convertible top that can be opened in good weather. The car is very fast. When it starts off, the Elan takes just seven seconds to reach 60 miles per hour (100 kph) . Like all modern sports cars, it is built low to the ground and has a sleek shape that can cut easily through the air.

The Elan is also a safe car. The lightweight plastic body is made strong by a steel body frame called the chassis. Steel beams in the doors help protect the driver and passenger from injury in an accident. A good suspension system keeps the car level around corners. Its large front disc brakes help the Elan stop quickly, even at high speeds.

3 The low hood and high rear deck give a smooth line from front to back, which helps the car cut through the air. This shape produces low drag, or air resistance, at high speeds.

1600 cc engine

1 The turbocharger forces extra air into the engine to make the fuel burn more quickly, which increases power.

2 The engine has four valves in each cylinder to increase engine power. Fuel can flow in and exhaust gases flow out more rapidly with four valves.

Engine drives front wheels

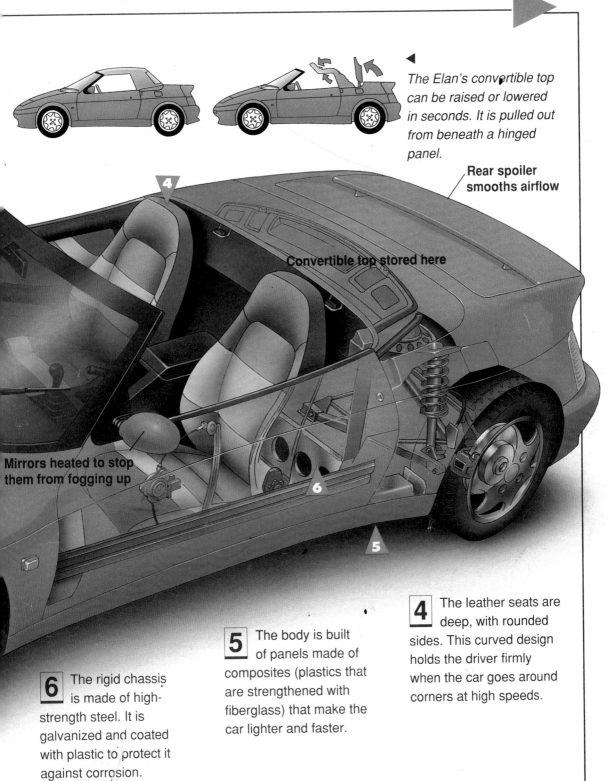

The Elan's convertible top can be raised or lowered in seconds. It is pulled out from beneath a hinged panel.

Rear spoiler smooths airflow

Convertible top stored here

Mirrors heated to stop them from fogging up

6 The rigid chassis is made of high-strength steel. It is galvanized and coated with plastic to protect it against corrosion.

5 The body is built of panels made of composites (plastics that are strengthened with fiberglass) that make the car lighter and faster.

4 The leather seats are deep, with rounded sides. This curved design holds the driver firmly when the car goes around corners at high speeds.

► U.S. Sports Car

Sports cars are usually smaller than family cars, with seats for only the driver and one passenger. These cars are built lower to the ground. They are sleek and often have a convertible top. In the United States, where cars are bigger than in Europe, sports cars are also bigger and more powerful.

The Chevrolet Corvette's 5.7-liter engine can drive the car as fast at 180 miles per hour (290 kph). It can also go from 0 to 60 miles per hour (96.6 kph) in 4.5 seconds.

2 The car's speed is controlled by the driver using the gearbox, which links the engine to the wheels. There are six different gears.

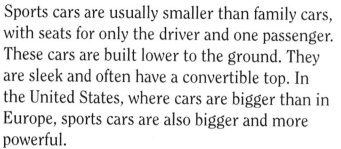

Brake light on the roof is easily seen in heavy traffic

1 The rear springs of most cars are made of steel, but the Corvette ZR-1's rear springs are made of fiberglass.

Four exhaust pipes, but two are fake

The extra wide tires were developed from Formula One racing tires.

3 The power for the car comes from an enormous engine. It has eight cylinders, with four valves to a cylinder.

4 As the ZR-1's speed builds up, computer-controlled motors make the suspension system increasingly stiff at higher speeds to help make the car's ride more steady.

The car is only 4 feet (102 m) at its highest point.

Engine designed by Lotus in England

Low tire pressure sensor lights a warning on the dashboard

5 The extra-wide tires are 9.5 inches (24 cm) wide at the front and 11 inches (28 cm) wide at the rear. The wide tires grip the road.

6 The Chevrolet Corvette is a rear-wheel drive car. This means that the engine turns the rear wheels.

The Corvette's headlights are usually hidden under covers. When a switch is touched, the covers flip up, and the headlights turn on.

▶ Super Car

Many sports cars can reach speeds of 150 miles per hour (240 kph), but there are some models which go much faster. These are called "super cars." Only a few hundred of each super car are built, and they are very expensive to buy. Because they are so fast, they can only be driven at their highest speeds on racetracks, not on open roads.

The Ferrari F40 is built in Italy. It can go as fast as 202 miles per hour (325 kph) and can go from 0 to 112 miles per hour (170 kph) in 12 seconds. Most cars have the engine in front of the driver. The F40's engine is behind the seat.

2 Oil for lubrication flows through a radiator behind the right rear wheel. It is cooled by air and then returned to the engine.

The car is less than 4 feet (1.2 m) high.

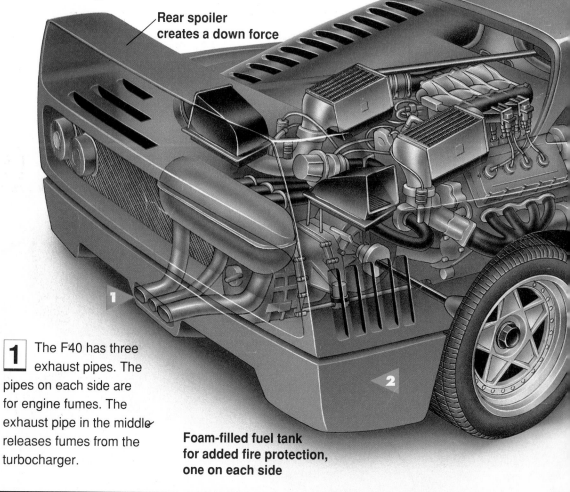

Rear spoiler creates a down force

1 The F40 has three exhaust pipes. The pipes on each side are for engine fumes. The exhaust pipe in the middle releases fumes from the turbocharger.

Foam-filled fuel tank for added fire protection, one on each side

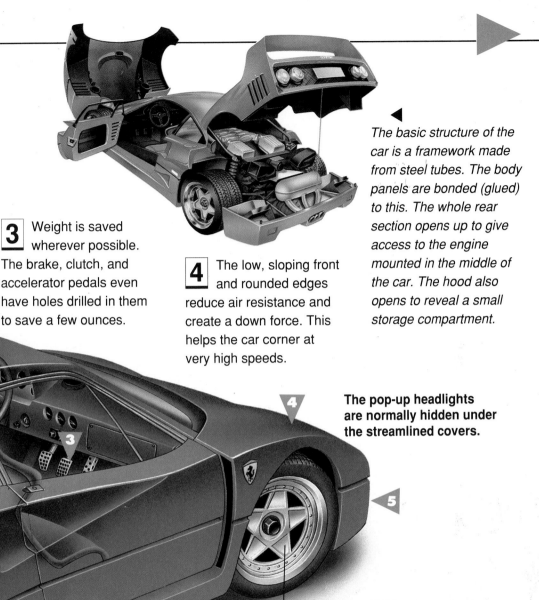

The basic structure of the car is a framework made from steel tubes. The body panels are bonded (glued) to this. The whole rear section opens up to give access to the engine mounted in the middle of the car. The hood also opens to reveal a small storage compartment.

3 Weight is saved wherever possible. The brake, clutch, and accelerator pedals even have holes drilled in them to save a few ounces.

4 The low, sloping front and rounded edges reduce air resistance and create a down force. This helps the car corner at very high speeds.

The pop-up headlights are normally hidden under the streamlined covers.

Alloy wheels

5 The outside of the car is made from 12 strong but lightweight carbon-fiber and fiberglass panels.

Fuel filler cap, one on each side

6 Two openings take in air. These are called "air ducts." The top duct cools the engine; the lower duct cools the rear brake.

Rally Car

The course for some races takes cars across the open country, high up on hills, and along forest roads. This type of race is called a "rally" and can last for several days. The cars that are used are ordinary production cars but with many extra features and more powerful engines. In these tough events the cars are driven as fast as possible, day and night, over long and winding courses. The roads are often very bumpy with loose dirt and stones.

The Nissan Sunny (Sentra) GTi-R is based on the standard Nissan Sunny (Sentra) three-door hatchback. It is smaller than most rally cars, but it has been very successful.

2 The wraparound seats have racing harnesses to hold the driver and codriver firmly in position at high speed.

Towing eyes —

1 The suspension normally fitted to the Sunny (Sentra) is not strong enough for rally driving. The rally car has a much tougher suspension.

Towing eyes
for pulling the car out of ditches

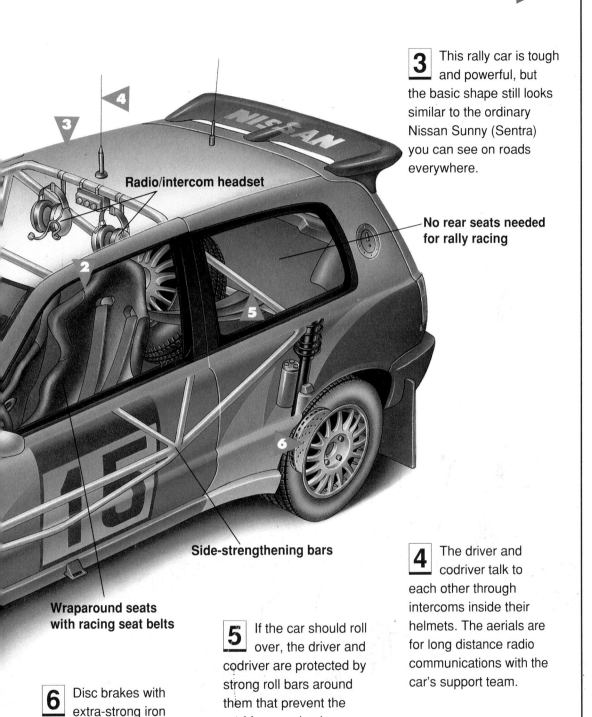

3 This rally car is tough and powerful, but the basic shape still looks similar to the ordinary Nissan Sunny (Sentra) you can see on roads everywhere.

Radio/intercom headset

No rear seats needed for rally racing

Side-strengthening bars

Wraparound seats with racing seat belts

4 The driver and codriver talk to each other through intercoms inside their helmets. The aerials are for long distance radio communications with the car's support team.

5 If the car should roll over, the driver and codriver are protected by strong roll bars around them that prevent the roof from caving in.

6 Disc brakes with extra-strong iron discs are fitted to stop the car safely and quickly at high speeds.

Endurance Racing Car

"Endurance races" can last 24 hours. Cars used in these races are very big and powerful.

The Peugeot 905 is an endurance racing car. Several drivers take turns driving the car at speeds up to 250 miles per hour (400 kph). During the Le Mans 24-hour race in France, the drivers change gears 18,000 times and cover more than 2,796 miles (4,500 km).

3 Air is mixed with fuel and burned inside the engine. The air is collected by a large scoop positioned above the cockpit.

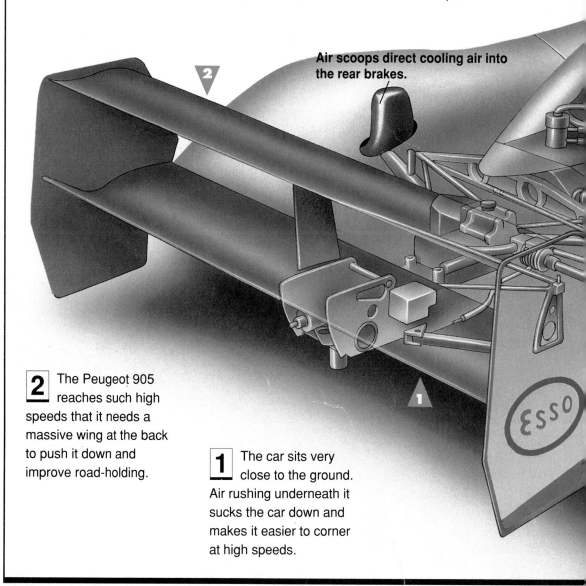

Air scoops direct cooling air into the rear brakes.

2 The Peugeot 905 reaches such high speeds that it needs a massive wing at the back to push it down and improve road-holding.

1 The car sits very close to the ground. Air rushing underneath it sucks the car down and makes it easier to corner at high speeds.

ESSO

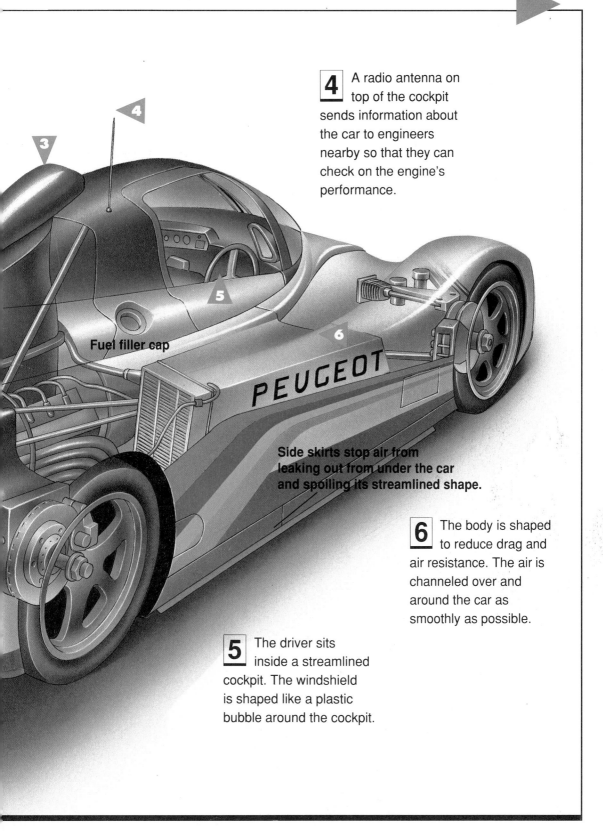

4 A radio antenna on top of the cockpit sends information about the car to engineers nearby so that they can check on the engine's performance.

Fuel filler cap

PEUGEOT

Side skirts stop air from leaking out from under the car and spoiling its streamlined shape.

6 The body is shaped to reduce drag and air resistance. The air is channeled over and around the car as smoothly as possible.

5 The driver sits inside a streamlined cockpit. The windshield is shaped like a plastic bubble around the cockpit.

Formula One Racing Car

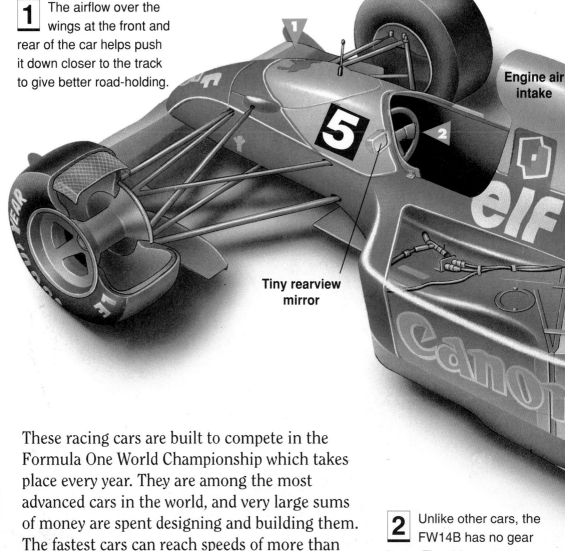

1 The airflow over the wings at the front and rear of the car helps push it down closer to the track to give better road-holding.

Engine air intake

Tiny rearview mirror

These racing cars are built to compete in the Formula One World Championship which takes place every year. They are among the most advanced cars in the world, and very large sums of money are spent designing and building them. The fastest cars can reach speeds of more than 218 miles per hour (350 kph).

One successful Formula One car is the Williams Renault FW14B, a car built in Great Britain with an engine made in France. It is the car that Nigel Mansell drove to win 9 of the 16 Formula One races. At the time, this was more than any other driver had won in a season to become Formula One World Champion.

2 Unlike other cars, the FW14B has no gear lever. The driver uses a faster transmission system that works by pressing buttons located on the steering wheel.

3 The car's power comes from a 302 pound (137 kg) engine. It is mounted behind the driver's head and drives the rear wheels.

4 Smooth tires called "slicks" keep more rubber touching the track. In wet weather, tires with treads are used. The treads push the water away from the tires.

5 An electronic system between the rear wheels stops them from spinning too much at the start of the race. This gives the car a fast get-away.

Streamlined engine cover

Air intake for cooling brakes

Rear wing

xtra-wide tires

6 A computer controls the suspension system to keep the car level while it is in a race. If the car is level, it can corner at higher speeds.

Glossary

Accelerator
The pedal inside the car that is pressed to make the car accelerate (increase in speed)

All-wheel drive
A vehicle with a transmission that delivers power to all four wheels

Aerodynamics
The study of how air flows around things. Aerodynamics are important in designing the shape of car bodies.

Anti-lock Braking System (ABS)
Computerized brakes that stop a car from skidding. A sensor detects when a wheel is about to skid, releases the brakes for a fraction of a second, and then reapplies them.

Body
The outer covering of a car that gives it its shape

Carbon fiber
Fine strands of carbon used to strengthen composite materials

Chassis
The basic framework of a car that gives it strength

Cockpit
The part of a racing car in which the driver sits

Composites
Materials made from plastic strengthened by strands of glass or carbon

Corrosion
The weakening and decay of metal parts by the action of weather — rusting, for example

Cylinder
A container inside a car engine where the fuel is burned. Car engines have four or more cylinders.

Diesel
A fuel oil, thicker than gasoline, used by vehicles with diesel engines

Disc brakes
Brakes that work by gripping a disc attached to the wheel to slow it down

Down force
The downward push on a car that helps it to grip the road and go around corners more quickly. Down force is produced by the effect of air flowing around a wing attached to the car.

Drag
Air resistance which slows a car down

Drum brakes
Brakes that work by pressing pads against a drum attached to the wheel to slow it down

Fiberglass
A strong yet lightweight material made from fine strands of glass set in hard plastic

Fuel
A material, such as gasoline, that is burned to release the energy stored inside it

Galvanized steel
Steel with a protective coating of a material, like zinc, to stop it from rusting

Gearbox
A set of gears that link the engine to the wheels and allows the car's speed to be varied smoothly

Hood
A hinged panel at the front of a car that opens up to reveal the engine or, if the engine is at the back of the car, a small luggage space

Lubrication
The use of a slippery material, like oil, to keep engine parts moving freely

Radiator
A device for getting rid of unwanted heat, thus keeping an engine cool. Hot water or oil flowing through fine tubes is cooled by blowing air around the tubes.

Road-holding
The ability of a car to grip the road

Steering column
The metal rod or shaft that connects a car's steering wheel to its front wheels

Streamlined
Smoothly shaped so that air can flow around easily

Suspension
A set of springs that help cushion a car from bumps in the road

Tailgate
The rear door of a car that usually opens upward for loading cargo

Turbocharger
A turbine driven by the engine's exhaust gases that forces air into the engine under pressure and boosts the engine power

Valve
A device inside an engine that lets gases flow in one direction only. One set of valves opens to let fuel and air into the engine cylinders, and a second set opens to let the exhaust gases out.

Wing
A curved panel on the front or rear of a car that acts like an upside-down aircraft wing. Air flowing around it sucks the car downward to give the car a better grip on the road.

▶ Index